What's in this book

This book belongs to

T0351525

_____

不一样的季节 Different seasons

学习内容 Contents

沟通 Communication

说说季节
Talk about the seasons

生词 New words

★ 冬天	winter
★ 夏天	summer
★ 已经	already
★ 春天	spring
★ 秋天	autumn
★ 非常	very
★ 一点儿	a few, a little
★ 云	cloud

背景介绍：
伊森、艾文和他们的好朋友威廉、米亚分别生活在地球的北半球和南半球。南北半球的季节刚好相反，当好朋友正在过夏天时，伊森和艾文正在过冬天。

米亚
（Mia）

威廉
（William）

啊	(used at the end of the sentence to express appreciation, doubt, urge, etc.)
最近	recently
空调	air conditioner
季节	season
暖和	warm
凉快	cool

文化 Cultures

冬至
The Winter Solstice Festival

句式 Sentence patterns

我们这里现在是夏天，最近
已经开空调了。
Since it is summer here, we
have already turned on the air-
conditioner.

跨学科学习 Project

介绍一座城市的气候
Introduce the climate of a city

参考答案：
1 I like spring/summer/autumn/winter best.
2 It is in winter/summer.
3 They are in winter.

Get ready

1 Which season do you like best?

2 Which season is Christmas in in your country?

3 Which season are Ethan and Ivan in?

wèi shén me bù lěng a
为什么不冷啊？

故事大意：
圣诞节，伊森、艾文与澳大利亚的好朋友视频聊天，惊讶地发现他们所处的季节并不相同，朋友向他们介绍了当地的季节特点。

"啊"用在句末，用来表示疑惑、惊叹等语气，如"你是谁啊？""真高啊！"

参考问题和答案：

1 Which country are William and Mia in? (They are in Australia, because they are holding Australia's national flag.)

2 Why does Ivan look so surprised? (Because it is winter in his country, but William and Mia are wearing summer clothes.)

"圣诞快乐！现在是冬天，你们为什么不冷啊？"艾文问。

"圣诞快乐！我们这里现在是夏天，
最近已经开空调了。"威廉说。

"真有趣！我们的季节不一样啊。春天和秋天呢？"伊森问。

fēi cháng nuǎn huo
非常暖和

"非常"是"很"的意思。

liáng kuai
凉快

参考问题和答案：

1 When is spring in Mia's country?
(It is from September to November.)

2 What is it like? (It is very warm.)

3 How about autumn? (It is from March to May. It is cool in autumn.)

"春天从九月开始，非常暖和。三月到五月是秋天，很凉快。"米亚说。

参考问题和答案：
What is the weather like at William's place? (It is sunny. There are a few clouds in the sky.)

"一点儿"表示很少或很小。

yǒu yī diǎnr yún
有一点儿云

"你们那里现在天气真好，天空只有一点儿云，很晴朗。"艾文说。

8

"快来找我们玩儿吧！过一个不一样的圣诞节。"米亚说。

Let's think

故事中米亚提到澳大利亚的秋天是三到五月，根据"春夏秋冬"的循环便可推断出冬天是六到八月。而米亚又说春天从九月开始，即春天是从九到十一月，剩下的十二月到二月便是夏天了。

1 Recall the story. When is summer and winter in William and Mia's country? Write the letters.

a 六月、七月、八月

b 十二月、一月、二月

六月、七月、八月

十二月、一月、二月

Summer

Winter

b

a

2 Do you prefer a winter Christmas or a summer Christmas? Discuss with your friend. 参考表达见下方。

夏天比冬天好，因为我可以……

夏天比冬天好，因为我可以和家人一起去游泳。游泳是很好的运动。

冬天比夏天好，因为我喜欢……

冬天比夏天好，因为我喜欢冬天。我也喜欢坐我的"小雪车"，它太可爱了！

New words

1 Learn the new words.

春天天气一点儿都不冷，很暖和，天上有一点儿云。

云

暖和

一点儿都不冷。

夏天天气非常热，我们已经开空调了。

空调

已经非常热了。

真凉快啊！

季节

春天　夏天

秋天　冬天

刮风了，秋天真凉快啊！

最近很冷。

最近开始下雪，今年冬天真冷。

2 Use the words above and the ones you have learnt to talk about the weather today.

听听说说 Listen and say

 1 Listen carefully. Put a tick or a cross.

1

✗

2
✗

3
✓

4
✓

 2 Look at the pictures. Listen to the story a

①

我是小熊。夏天非常热，天空没有一点儿云，我爱和小鱼去游泳。

③

冬天，下雪了。天气很冷，我在家里休息。

第二题参考问题和答案：
1 In which season does the bear go to sleep? (In winter.)
2 What do you like to do during your favourite season?
(My favourite season is autumn/winter. I like to fly kites/build snowmen.)

3 Talk about the pictures with your friend.

现在是什么季节？

现在已经是……了，天气……

秋天真凉快。我喜欢和朋友们一起跑跑跳跳。

天气真暖和啊！红的花，绿的草。春天已经来了！

1

参考表达：
现在已经是冬天了，天气很冷，最近开始下雪了。

2

现在已经是春天了，天气很暖和。树上的花非常好看。

3

现在已经是秋天了，天气真凉快、真舒服。

Task

What is your friends' favourite activity in each of the four seasons? Do a survey and report your results.

活动 ＼ 季节	春天	夏天	秋天	冬天
打篮球				
踢足球				
跑步				
骑自行车				
游泳				

春天你最喜欢做什么?

春天我最喜欢……

春天喜欢……的人最多。

Game

游戏方法：
老师每次挑选一个季节和花朵上的若干词汇，学生发挥创意，用这些词汇说一段话。

Listen to the words your teacher says and use them to make sentences.

春天、太阳、暖和、冷。

春天不冷，有太阳，很暖和。

太阳　晴天　暖和　空调　冷

热　凉快　云　下雪　下雨　刮风

春天　夏天　秋天　冬天

Chant

Listen and say. 说唱前让学生先将第3至6句话与图片配对。其中第3句对左上图，第4句对右上图。第5句对左下图，第6句对右下图。

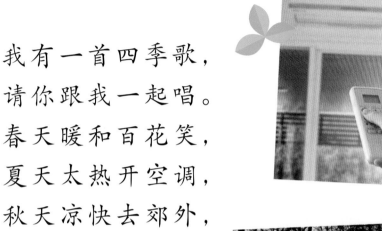

我有一首四季歌，
请你跟我一起唱。
春天暖和百花笑，
夏天太热开空调，
秋天凉快去郊外，
冬天很冷多睡觉。
春夏秋冬各不同，
四季变化真奇妙。

生活用语 Daily expressions

参考对话见下方。

不用了，谢谢。
No, thanks.

我没事儿。
I am OK.

叔叔：吃蛋糕吗？
女孩：不用了，谢谢。

姐姐：疼吗？
男孩：我没事儿。

写一写 Write

1 Trace and write the characters.

一 二 三 声 夫 夫 春 春 春

春 春 春

提醒学生"春"字的第二横要比
第一横短，第三横是最长的。

一 二 千 千 禾 禾 秒 秋

秋 秋 秋

丿 夂 冬 冬 冬

冬 冬 冬

2 Write and say.

他们非常喜欢 冬 天，因为
可以玩雪。

这里 春 天暖和， 秋 天凉快。

告诉学生通过找关键词确定答案的答题技巧。选择正确答案前，先让学生通读段落，再划出段落中的关键词：绿树红花、秋天、夏天、热。通过"秋天"和"夏天"可以初步猜测该段落是关于"季节"的；"绿树红花"是"春天"的景象；"秋天"的天气一般都比较"凉快"；"夏天"通常会"非常""热"。

3 Read and circle the correct words.

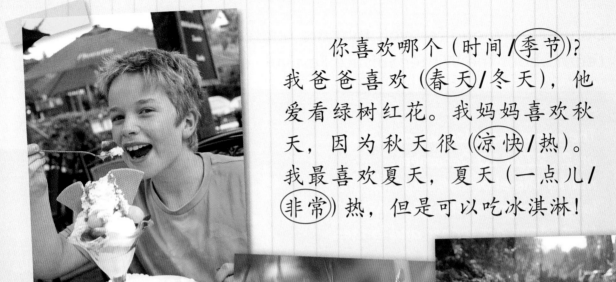

你喜欢哪个（时间/(季节)）?

我爸爸喜欢（(春天)/冬天），他爱看绿树红花。我妈妈喜欢秋天，因为秋天很（(凉快)/热）。我最喜欢夏天，夏天（一点儿/(非常)）热，但是可以吃冰淇淋！

通过此题让学生了解一段话必须有一个明确的主题。首先让学生看看图片和段落第一句话，发现这一段话是关于一个女孩的。接着让他们找出两句不相关的句子，即第二句（写"我"）和第四句（写"北京"），这两句即为答案。

拼音输入法 Pinyin input

Read the paragraph and cross out the two irrelevant sentences. Then type the correct paragraph.

这个女孩是我的朋友。~~我有五个好朋友。~~她是中国人，但是她会说英语。她的家在上海。~~北京比上海大。~~上海现在是夏天，最近非常热。她喜欢和她的小狗在花园玩，因为花园里很凉快。

多元学习 Connections

Cultures   北半球的冬至在每年公历的 12 月 21 日至 23 日。冬至这天是全年夜晚最长的一天，此后，夜晚逐渐缩短，白天逐渐变长。由此，中国人认为冬至是"阴"和"阳"交替的节点。

1 Do you know any festivals that are related to the seasons? Learn about the Winter Solstice Festival celebrated in China.

下图从最上方开始，按顺时针顺序，依次为春分，冬至，秋分，夏至。

> 今天白天 (day) 最短，夜晚 (night) 最长。

The winter solstice, which occurs on 21, 22 or 23 December, marks the shortest day and the longest night of the year. After that, days get longer and longer.

spring equinox

Sun

summer solstice

winter solstice

autumn equinox

The ancient Chinese celebrated the Winter Solstice Festival (冬至) for the 'return' of the sun. Today it is a day for family reunion. Dumplings and glutinous rice balls are the most popular foods eaten on this day.

冬至北方有吃饺子、南方有吃汤圆的习俗，传说吃了饺子不冻人，吃汤圆则象征家庭和谐、吉祥。

2 Australia is in the southern hemisphere. Which date would its winter solstice occur on? Discuss with your friend and circle it.

参考表达见下方。

> 它的冬天从……月开始，所以……

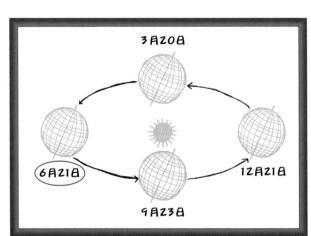

3月20日

6月21日

12月21日

9月23日

它的冬天从六月开始，所以它的冬至不在九月、十二月和三月。
它的冬至在六月二十一日，那天白天最短，夜晚最长。

1 Did you know that climates vary around the world? Take a look at the climates of some places around the world.

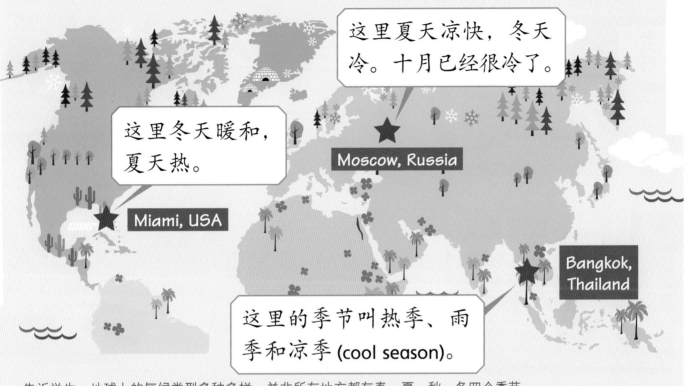

这里夏天凉快，冬天冷。十月已经很冷了。

这里冬天暖和，夏天热。

Moscow, Russia

Miami, USA

Bangkok, Thailand

这里的季节叫热季、雨季和凉季 (cool season)。

告诉学生，地球上的气候类型多种多样，并非所有地方都有春、夏、秋、冬四个季节。

2 Paste a photo of your favourite city and introduce it to your friend. Talk about its climate and suggest the best time to visit.

Paste your photo here.

这是……（城市）。

……（季节）是从……月到……月。

……天来这里玩最好，因为天气……

温习 Checkpoint

延伸活动：
学生在教室内模仿下图共同制作一面展览墙。学生可以按季节和月份将照片或自己画的画贴在展览墙上，与同学共同分享四季的乐趣。

1 The children are decorating the classroom wall with photos of the four seasons. Read the captions and write the characters. Then draw pictures and talk about them.

春 天

三月

五月

四月

最近有一点儿热。

夏天

已经是夏天了！

六月

七月

有空调，真凉快。

八月

秋 天

天真蓝啊，没有云。

九月

十月

十一月

冬 天

一月

外面非常冷。

二月

十二月

家里很暖和。

2 Work with your friend. Colour the stars and the chillies.

Words	说	读	写
冬天	☆	☆	🌶
夏天	☆	☆	🌶
已经	☆	☆	🌶
春天	☆	☆	🌶
秋天	☆	☆	🌶
非常	☆	☆	🌶
一点儿	☆	☆	🌶
云	☆	☆	🌶
啊	☆	🌶	🌶
最近	☆	🌶	🌶

Words and sentences	说	读	写
空调	☆	🌶	🌶
季节	☆	🌶	🌶
暖和	☆	🌶	🌶
凉快	☆	🌶	🌶
我们这里现在是夏天，最近已经开空调了。	☆	🌶	🌶

Talk about the seasons	☆

3 What does your teacher say?

My teacher says ...

分享 Sharing

Words I remember

冬天	dōng tiān	winter
夏天	xià tiān	summer
已经	yǐ jīng	already
春天	chūn tiān	spring
秋天	qiū tiān	autumn
非常	fēi cháng	very
一点儿	yī diǎnr	a few, a little
云	yún	cloud
啊	a	(used at the end of the sentence to express appreciation, doubt, urge, etc.)

延伸活动：
1 学生用手遮盖英文，读中文单词，并思考单词意思；
2 学生用手遮盖中文单词，看着英文说出对应的中文单词；
3 学生四人一组，尽量运用中文单词分角色复述故事。

最近	zuì jìn	recently
空调	kōng tiáo	air conditioner
季节	jì jié	season

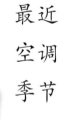

| 暖和 | nuǎn huo | warm |
| 凉快 | liáng kuai | cool |

Other words

圣诞（节）	shèng dàn (jié)	Christmas
有趣	yǒu qù	interesting
一样	yī yàng	same
从	cóng	from
到	dào	to
天空	tiān kōng	sky
只	zhǐ	only
晴朗	qíng lǎng	sunny
快	kuài	quickly
找	zhǎo	to call on
过	guò	to spend

OXFORD
UNIVERSITY PRESS

Oxford University Press is a department of the University of Oxford.
It furthers the University's objective of excellence in research, scholarship,
and education by publishing worldwide. Oxford is a registered trade mark of
Oxford University Press in the UK and in certain other countries

Published in Hong Kong by
Oxford University Press (China) Limited
39th Floor, One Kowloon, 1 Wang Yuen Street, Kowloon Bay,
Hong Kong

© Oxford University Press (China) Limited 2017

The moral rights of the author have been asserted

First Edition published in 2017

Illustrated by Anne Lee, KY Chan and Wildman

Photographs for reproduction permitted by Dreamstime.com

China National Publications Import & Export (Group) Corporation is an authorized distributor of
Oxford Elementary Chinese.

Please contact content@cnpiec.com.cn or 86-10-65856782

ISBN: 978-0-19-047008-1

10 9 8 7 6 5 4 3 2

Teacher's Edition
ISBN: 978-0-19-082316-0

10 9 8 7 6 5 4 3 2